KU-575-583

WHY DO I GET SUNBURN?

✦ and other questions about skin ✦

Heinemann
LIBRARY

Angela Royston

www.heinemann.co.uk/library

Visit our website to find out more information about **Heinemann Library** books.

To order:

 Phone 44 (0) 1865 888066

 Send a fax to 44 (0) 1865 314091

 Visit the Heinemann Bookshop at www.heinemann.co.uk/library to browse our catalogue and order online.

First published in Great Britain by Heinemann Library, Halley Court, Jordan Hill, Oxford OX2 8EJ, a division of Reed Educational and Professional Publishing Ltd. Heinemann is a registered trademark of Reed Educational & Professional Publishing Limited.

OXFORD MELBOURNE AUCKLAND JOHANNESBURG BLANTYRE
GABORONE IBADAN PORTSMOUTH NH (USA) CHICAGO

© Reed Educational and Professional Publishing Ltd 2002
The moral right of the proprietor has been asserted.

All rights reserved. No part of this publication may be reproduced, stored in a retrieval system, or transmitted in any form or by any means, electronic, mechanical, photocopying, recording, or otherwise without either the prior written permission of the Publishers or a licence permitting restricted copying in the United Kingdom issued by the Copyright Licensing Agency Ltd, 90 Tottenham Court Road, London W1P 0LP.

Designed by Joanna Sapwell and StoryBooks
Illustrations by Nick Hawken
Originated by Ambassador Litho Ltd
Printed in China by South China Printing Company

06 05 04 03 02
10 9 8 7 6 5 4 3 2 1

ISBN 0 431 11078 6

DUDLEY PUBLIC LIBRARIES

L   46611

640609   SCH

J612.79

British Library Cataloguing in Publication Data
Royston, Angela
Why do I get sunburn?.– (Body matters)
1. Sunburn – Juvenile literature
I.Title
612.7'9

Acknowledgements
The Publishers would like to thank the following for permission to reproduce photographs:
Action Plus: 16; BSIP: 14; Corbis: 5; Gareth Boden: 8, 9, 20, 22, 24, 25, 28; Powerstock/Zefa: 11, 17, 18, 19, 27; Science Photo Library: 6, 10, 21; Stone: 4, 13; Tudor Photography: 15.

Cover photograph reproduced with permission of Powerstock/Zefa.

Our thanks to Anne Long for her help in the preparation of this book.

Every effort has been made to contact copyright holders of any material reproduced in this book. Any omissions will be rectified in subsequent printings if notice is given to the Publisher.

CONTENTS

Words printed in **bold letters like these** are explained in the Glossary.

WHAT DOES MY SKIN DO?

Skin is an all-over protection suit. It separates and protects the inside of your body from the world outside. It stops dirt, germs and other harmful things, such as the Sun's rays, getting into the body. It also stops moisture that is inside the body from getting out. The insides of your body are very moist and, without skin they would quickly dry out.

Germs

Germs are **bacteria** and **viruses** that attack parts of your body and make you ill. Some germs do get inside your body when you eat and drink and breathe in air. The rest of your body, however, is protected by skin. If you cut or graze your skin, you have to clean the wound and cover it to keep out dirt and germs.

This girl's skin is covered in mud. The mud won't harm her because her skin will stop any dirt or germs from getting inside her body, but she will need to wash!

Burns

You can see how important skin is by looking at what happens when some of it is lost by being burnt or scalded. Burns are caused by some chemicals and by electricity as well as by flames. Very hot liquid and steam scalds the skin. If you touch something that is too hot, you will get a mild but painful burn. Small, light burns heal themselves, but large or deep burns must be treated in hospital. Serious burns destroy the skin. This makes it easy for germs to get inside the body. The burns must be treated quickly, so the body does not dry out.

Skin is waterproof. It stops water leaking into and out of your body.

WHY DOES MY SKIN FLAKE?

If your skin becomes very dry, it becomes flaky. Skin is made up of two layers – the **dermis** and the **epidermis**. Both consist of millions of tiny **cells**, but the cells in the outer layer, the epidermis, are all dead. These dead cells are tough and hard to protect you against knocks and scrapes. As they gradually flake off they are replaced by new cells from the dermis below. Dead cells flake off all the time but they are usually so small you are not aware of them. In fact most of the dust in your home consists of flakes of dead skin!

This photo shows what the surface of the skin looks like through a microscope. You can see the flakes of dead skin.

Inside the skin

Skin consists of much more than skin cells. It contains **glands** that produce sweat or oil, and the roots of your hair and your nails. Tiny tubes of blood thread their way through the skin, bringing food and oxygen to all the living cells. **Nerve endings** tell your brain what your skin is feeling.

Hair

Long, thick hair grows from your scalp, the skin that covers your head. Fine hairs cover most of the rest of your skin, except the palms of your hand and the soles of your feet. An oil gland just below the epidermis makes oil that keeps each hair soft and bendy.

A TYPICAL SQUARE CENTIMETRE OF SKIN CONTAINS:

- 15 hairs
- 15 oil glands
- 100 sweat glands
- 55 cm of nerves
- 500,000 dead and dying cells.

A magnified drawing of the inside of your skin.

hair

sweat pore

nerve endings

sweat gland

blood vessel

epidermis

dermis

oil gland

hair root

fat

HOW THICK SKINNED AM I?

Your skin varies in thickness on different parts of your body. The thickest skin is on the soles of your feet where it is about 5 mm thick. If you walk around in bare feet a lot, the **epidermis** will become even thicker – up to 10 mm thick. The epidermis contains a special substance called **keratin**, which makes the outer skin **cells** hard and tough.

Thin skin

Your skin is thinnest on your eyelids. Here it is only 1–2 mm thick. It is so thin that you can see a change from light to dark with your eyes closed. You can test this by shining a torch on your closed eyes and turning the torch off and on.

Gravel hurts your feet, but some people have such a thick layer of skin on their feet they can walk over gravel and rocks without feeling any pain.

Hard pads

If you do something that continually rubs part of your skin, the epidermis will become thicker there. If you like swinging from monkey bars, for example, thick pads of hard skin called calluses will form on the palms of your hand, just below your fingers.

Blisters

A blister protects your skin when it is rubbed away too quickly for the skin below to replace the lost cells. For example, you may get blisters if you go on a long walk and your shoes rub the back of your heels. The shoes rub away the top layer of skin so that the delicate layer of living skin below is unprotected. A blister contains liquid that cushions the skin below.

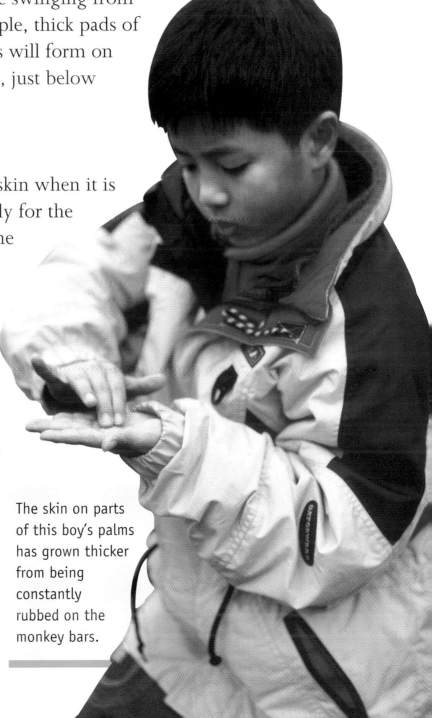

The skin on parts of this boy's palms has grown thicker from being constantly rubbed on the monkey bars.

WHY DO I GET SUNBURN?

The Sun's rays contain harmful **radiation** that can damage **cells** in the body. Skin protects the body from radiation but it can get burnt in the process.

Too much sun

The skin can only withstand a certain amount of radiation. If it is exposed to too much sunshine, it becomes red and sore. If the burn is mild, the redness fades in a few hours. But if it is severe, the skin may become swollen and peel off before the burn fades. Too much sunshine can also make you feel sick, weak and dizzy. You may even get a fever, which is when your temperature becomes higher than normal.

This man has spent too long in the sunshine and is sunburnt. The red skin will feel hot and sore later.

Strongest sunshine

The Sun's rays are strongest when they are most directly overhead. This means that they are strongest in summer and from the late morning until the middle of the afternoon. But the Sun's rays can still harm you at other times of the day and year. The Sun's rays are stronger the nearer you are to the equator (an imaginary line drawn around the centre of the Earth, halfway between the North and South Poles).

Protecting yourself from the Sun

The best way to protect your skin from the Sun is to keep it covered. You should protect your back and chest by always wearing a shirt or T-shirt. Protect your head with a sunhat and your eyes with sunglasses. Rub any bare skin with sun protection cream. The Sun's rays travel through cloud and through water, so you must still protect your skin on cloudy days and when you are swimming.

Sun block protects your skin from the sun. Remember to rub in more cream after an hour or two and after swimming.

Melanin

The body has its own defence against the Sun's rays. Inside your skin are **cells** that produce **melanin**, a substance that absorbs the **radiation**. As the Sun shines on your skin, it makes more melanin. This makes your skin go darker because melanin is the substance that gives it its colour. The more melanin you have in your skin the better protected you are from the sun.

Skin colour

Some people are born with more melanin in their skin than others. The colour of human skin varies from black through all shades of brown to yellow, pink and white. You inherit your skin colour from your parents and, the more melanin you have, the darker your skin will be.

Special cells in the skin called melanocytes produce melanin. The melanin spreads throughout the **epidermis**.

grains of melanin in epidermis

melanocyte

Safe tanning

The Sun's rays are so damaging that you cannot rely only on your natural melanin. Some people with red hair and fair skin burn very easily. Without sun protection cream, light-skinned people should spend no more than 15 minutes a day in the Sun at first, and increase the time slowly, by 10 to 15 minutes a day. Using sun protection cream allows you to stay in the Sun longer than your skin's natural protection allows, but remember to apply the cream before you go into the Sun and reapply it every few hours.

People have different colours of skin, depending on whether they have a lot of melanin or only a little.

SUN PROTECTION CREAM

The sun protection factor tells you how long you can stay in the Sun.

- Factor 2 twice as long as normal
- Factor 6 six times as long as normal
- Factor 12 12 times as long as normal
- Factor 18 18 times as long as normal

WHAT ARE FRECKLES?

Freckles are small spots of darker skin, usually on the face and sometimes on the arms and hands. The number of freckles increases during the summer, when they also become darker. Freckles form where there is more **melanin** in the skin.

Melanocytes

The cells that produce melanin are called melanocytes. Everyone has roughly the same number of them but some people's melanocytes produce more melanin than other people's. People with white and fair skin have melanocytes that produce very little melanin. People with black or darker skin have melanocytes that produce lots of melanin. Freckles are small patches of skin that have extra melanin.

This boy has freckles across his nose and over his cheeks. They increase in the summer and fade in the winter.

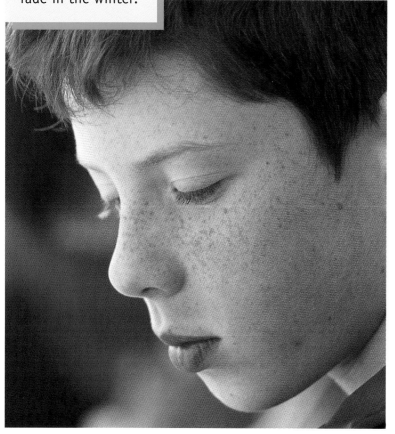

Moles

A mole is a patch of dark skin. It may be raised or flat and is caused by **cells** that contain melanin. Some moles may be present at birth but most appear while you are a child. Moles tend to run in families and are very common: most adults have about 40 moles. Moles are harmless, but occasionally a mole may become unhealthy. If you have a mole that hurts or bleeds, or changes suddenly, then you should see a doctor.

Birthmarks

Birthmarks are patches of skin that may be raised or flat and are present from birth. Some are called port wine stains, others are known as strawberry marks. They are made by large **blood vessels** close to the surface of the skin. Strawberry marks usually disappear on their own. Dark port wine stains can be made lighter by being treated with laser beams.

This person has several moles on their arm. Moles stay the same all year round.

WHY DO I GO RED WHEN I AM TOO HOT?

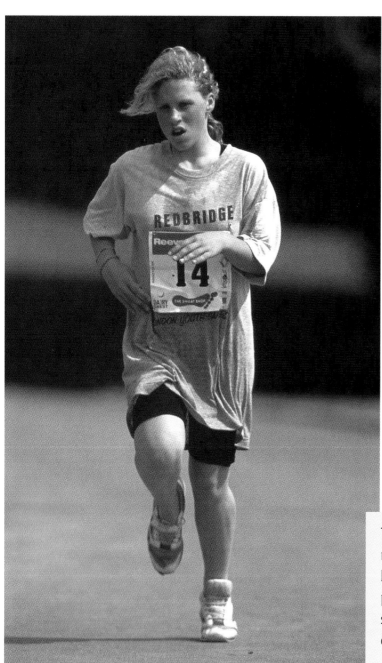

You often go red when you have been running or exercising. Muscles make heat and the heat is taken around the body by your blood. When you are hot, the tiny **blood vessels** in the skin become wider. This allows more blood to come to the surface of the body where it cools down, but the extra blood makes your skin look red.

This girl's face is red and hot. Extra blood is being pumped into the skin where it can cool down faster.

Sweating

When you are hot, sweat **glands** in the skin pump out extra sweat. Salty water then covers your skin and helps to cool you down. As it dries, it takes heat from your body and turns this into water vapour. Every part of your skin contains sweat glands and they lose moisture all the time, but you usually do not notice. Some parts of the body, such as the armpits, contain more sweat glands than other parts. As sweat **evaporates**, it leaves behind salt and a substance called urea. You need to wash regularly so that these salts do not clog the skin or cause you to become smelly.

Heat control

Part of the brain, called the hypothalamus, stops your body temperature getting too high or too low. When the temperature of your blood changes, it takes action. When the blood is too hot, it sends signals to the sweat glands and the blood vessels in the skin.

Tennis players and other athletes make so much sweat their shirts become soaked.

SWEAT

The body usually produces between 0.5 and 1 litre of sweat a day. The palms of the hands, the soles of the feet and the forehead produce the most sweat.

WHAT CAUSES GOOSEBUMPS?

When you are cold the hairs on your skin stand up. They do this to trap air close to your skin to help to keep you warm. Each hair has a tiny muscle in the skin that tenses to pull the hair up. Goosebumps are the hard bumps made by these tiny, tense muscles. This is like a bird fluffing its feathers to trap air when it is cold.

Shivering

When you are cold, your body shivers. The muscles work together to make you tremble. As your lower jaw shivers, your teeth close and unclose rapidly, making a chattering sound. Muscles make heat as they work, so shivering helps to warm you up.

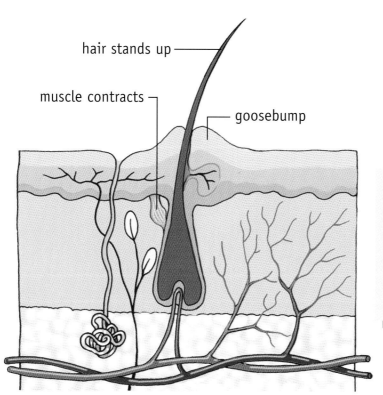

hair stands up

muscle contracts

goosebump

Goosebumps help to warm you up when you are cold by making the fine hairs on your skin stand up.

Pale skin

Your body also acts to stop heat escaping from it. Most heat is lost through your skin so the tiny **blood vessels** in your skin become narrower. This means that less blood comes into the skin and your skin looks much paler. If your feet or hands become very cold, they may become numb so that they cannot feel things properly. This is because the blood vessels have become so narrow, very little blood is reaching them. Stamping your feet and rubbing your hands will help to bring more blood to them.

Keeping warm

When the temperature of your blood drops, goosebumps, shivering and the blood vessels in your skin all work together to make you warmer. Putting on warmer clothes and having a warm drink also help to warm you up when you are cold.

When the weather is very cold you must dress up warmly. Make sure that your head, feet and hands are well protected from the cold and wet.

WHY DOES HAIR GROW THICKEST ON MY HEAD?

Hair keeps your head warm and plays an important part in how you look. Whether you plait your hair or have it loose, whether you have a fringe or not changes your appearance.

The long hairs that grow from your scalp help to keep you and your head warm. The body can lose a lot of heat through the scalp and so hair acts like an animal's hairy coat to keep heat in. In particular, the brain, below the scalp, needs to be warm for it to work well.

How hair grows

Hair is made of dead **cells** and contains a strong substance called **keratin**. This is the same substance that makes your nails hard and the outer layer of skin tough. New hair cells form in the root of the hair, in a pocket called a **follicle**, in the skin. As new cells are made, the older cells above them are pushed up through the skin to form the hair that you see. The hairs on your head grow about 1 mm every three days, or about 1 cm every month. Each individual hair grows only for about six years before it drops out.

Baldness

After a hair has dropped out, the hair root rests for about three or four months and then starts to grow a new hair. Some men become bald as, one by one, their hair roots stop producing new hairs. Baldness tends to run in families.

COUNTING HAIRS

You have about 100,000 to 120,000 hair follicles on your scalp. About 30 to 60 hairs fall out every day.

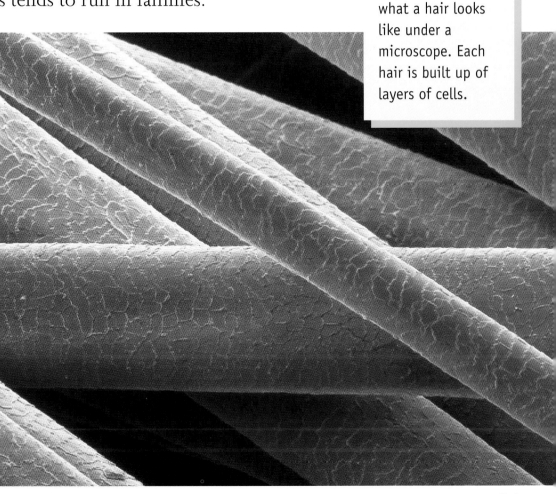

This photo shows what a hair looks like under a microscope. Each hair is built up of layers of cells.

WHY DO PEOPLE HAVE DIFFERENT COLOURED HAIR?

Black is the most common hair colour, but hair can be brown, different shades of red, blonde, grey or white. **Melanin** gives your hair its colour. The more melanin your body makes, the darker your hair will be. People with blonde or fair hair have very little melanin. Those with red or brown hair have some melanin but not as much as people with black hair.

These children have different coloured hair. You inherit your natural hair colour from your parents.

Changing the colour of hair

Some people change the colour of their hair by dyeing it or bleaching it. Hair dye gives hair a different colour, while bleaching removes the natural colour. As people grow old their hair may change colour naturally. The hair loses its colour and becomes grey or white.

follicle

follicle

follicle

Straight or curly?

Whether your hair is straight, wavy or curly depends on the shape of the **follicles** that the hairs grow from. Straight hair grows from round follicles, while wavy and curly hair grow from oval and from flat follicles. The flatter the follicle, the curlier the hair. Some people use chemicals to change their hair. Straight hair can be permed to make it curlier, and curly hair can be straightened.

Looking after your hair

You need to wash your hair regularly to keep it clean. You also need to cut off the ends from time to time, even if you are growing your hair. The end of a hair is the oldest part of it and after a while it tends to split. Trimming off the ends stops them splitting.

How straight or curly your hair is depends on the shape of the hair follicles in your scalp.

WHY DOESN'T IT HURT WHEN I CUT MY NAILS?

Cutting your nails does not hurt because there are no nerves in the nails. Like your hair, your nails are made of dead **cells** and contain **keratin**. This is the substance that makes them tough and hard. Nails are flat, horny plates that protect the ends of your fingers and toes. They give your fingertip something to press against to help you pick up very small items, such as pins or grains of rice.

How nails grow

New nail cells are made in the **nailbed** in the skin. As new cells are made, the older cells above them are pushed up through the skin.

A nail grows from special cells in the nailbed near the ends of the fingers and toes.

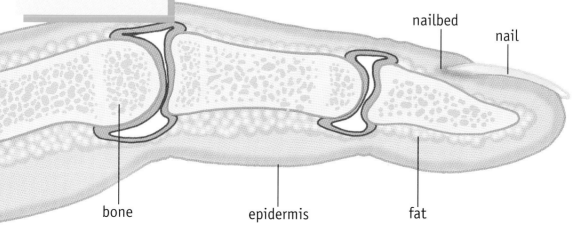

nailbed

nail

bone

epidermis

fat

24

Nails are white but look pink where the **epidermis** is so thin the **blood vessels** below show through. Cutting the white tip of the nail does not hurt, but if the pink part of the nail breaks the skin below hurts.

Cutting your nails

Keeping your nails cut short stops dirt getting trapped under them. Fingernails are usually cut or filed to a smooth, round shape, but it is better to cut toenails straight across. This helps to stop a painful, ingrowing toenail caused by the nail growing into the flesh at the side of the nail.

It is a good idea to keep your nails smooth and short so that they do not break easily. Use nail clippers or an emery board. Do not bite or pick your nails!

HOW FAST DO NAILS GROW?

Fingernails grow faster than toenails. Fingernails grow about 3 mm a month which is about 3.5 cm a year. Most people's nails break before they grow very long.

WHICH PART OF MY SKIN IS MOST SENSITIVE?

Different parts of the body are sensitive to different things. For example, bath water feels hotter to your feet than it does to your hand. But, if you wanted to feel how rough or smooth something is, you would feel it with your fingertips, not the back of your hand. If someone pinches you on the back, it won't feel as painful as if they pinched your arm.

Skin contains nerve endings that tell you how hot or cold something is and what it feels like.

Nerves in the skin

You feel things in your skin because it contains different kinds of **nerve endings**. One kind of nerve ending reacts to heat, while another kind reacts to cold. Three different kinds react to light touch, heavy pressure and pain. An area of skin that has a lot of one particular kind of nerve ending is sensitive to that thing.

heat   light touch   pain   pressure   cold

Fingertips

Your fingertips are particularly sensitive to light touch. You use your fingers to pick up small objects, to write and to tap the keys of a phone or computer. People with large hands and big fingers are usually better at doing fiddly things, such as threading a needle or doing up small buttons, than people with thin fingers. The ridged pattern of skin on the tips of the fingers makes them even more sensitive. If this ridged skin is damaged, the fingertips are much less sensitive.

FINGERTIPS

No two people have the same pattern of ridges so no one has the same fingerprints as you. Even identical twins have different fingerprints.

People who cannot see can read books printed in braille. In braille, each letter is shown by a pattern of dots that the person feels with their fingertips.

Lips and tongue

Your lips and tongue are packed with each kind of **nerve ending**. This makes them especially sensitive to hot and cold food and to touch and pain. If you bite your tongue by mistake, you will know how painful it is. And, when a tooth falls out, the gap left behind feels enormous to your tongue, but does not appear so large when you check in a mirror.

Pain

Pain protects your skin from harm. If you felt no pain, you would not realise when your skin and flesh was being burnt, cut or damaged. All parts of the body except the hair and nails contain nerve endings that react to pain. They tell you when there is something wrong. For example, your throat hurts when you are ill, and it hurts to move your hand when your wrist is broken.

This boy carefully sips a cup of hot chocolate. He uses his lips to tell how hot it is so that he does not burn his mouth.

BODY MAP

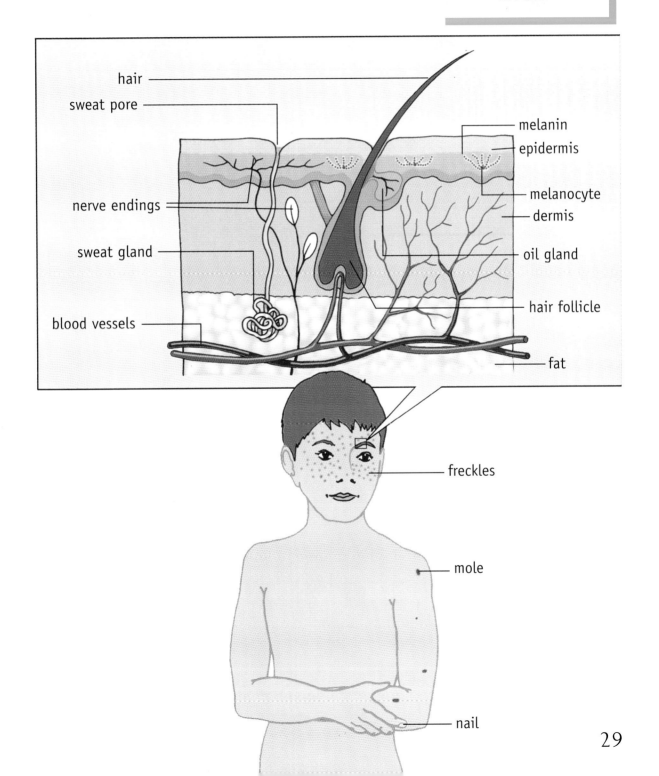

hair

sweat pore

melanin

epidermis

nerve endings

melanocyte

dermis

sweat gland

oil gland

hair follicle

blood vessels

fat

freckles

mole

nail

GLOSSARY

bacteria tiny living things. Some kinds of bacteria are germs that cause disease.

blood vessels tubes through which blood moves around the body

cells smallest building blocks of living things. The body has many kinds of cells, including skin cells, blood cells and hair cells.

dermis layer of skin beneath the epidermis

epidermis tough, outer layer of skin

evaporate turn from liquid, for example water, into gas or vapour

follicle small pocket in the skin from which a hair grows

germ bacteria or virus that makes you ill

glands parts of the body that produce particular substances such as sweat and saliva

keratin chemical substance that makes skin, nails and hair strong and hard

melanin chemical produced by the body and responsible for skin, hair and eye colour

nailbed part of the skin from which a nail grows

nerve ending these receive messages that tell the brain what the skin feels

radiation rays of energy from the Sun

virus a kind of germ that is even smaller than bacteria

FURTHER READING

Young Discoverers: Inside the Body, Sally Morgan, 1997, Kingfisher Books

I know how to fight germs, Kate Rowan, 2000, Walker Books

The Human Body Big Book, Penny Coltman, 1999, Longman

First Encyclopedia of the Human Body, 2001, Kingfisher Books

INDEX

Titles in the *Body Matters* series include:

Hardback   0431 11075 1

Hardback   0431 11073 5

Hardback   0431 11077 8

Hardback   0431 11078 6

Hardback   0431 11076 X

Hardback   0431 11070 0

Hardback   0431 11072 7

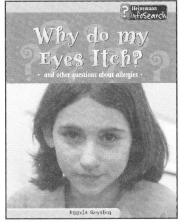

Hardback   0431 11071 9

Find out about the other titles in this series on our website www.heinemann.co.uk/library